THIS BOOK BELONGS TO...

FOOTBALL CLUB

Name: _____ Age: _____

Favourite player: _____

2023/24

My Predictions	Actual
The Blues' final position:	
The Blues' top scorer:	
Championship winners:	
Championship top scorer:	
FA Cup winners:	
EFL Cup winners:	

Contributors: Peter Rogers

A TWOCAN PUBLICATION

©2023. Published by twocan under licence from Ipswich Town Football Club.

Every effort has been made to ensure the accuracy of information within this publication but the publishers cannot be held responsible for any errors or omissions. Views expressed are those of the authors and do not necessarily represent those of the publishers or the football club. All rights reserved.

978-1-915571-58-8

PICTURE CREDITS: MatchDay Images, Paul Macro, Action Images, Alamy and Press Association

CONTENTS

THE CHAMPIONSHIP
SQUAD
2023/24

Christian
WALTON

1

POSITION: Goalkeeper **COUNTRY:** England **DOB:** 09/11/1995

Goalkeeper Christian Walton initially joined the Blues on loan from Premier League Brighton & Hove Albion in August 2021. The move became a permanent one in the 2022 January transfer window following a string of impressive performances. Ever-present in Town's promotion from League One in 2022/23, Walton was injured in training ahead of the club's current Championship campaign with all at Portman Road keen to see him swiftly back in action as the Ipswich Town's reliable last line of defence.

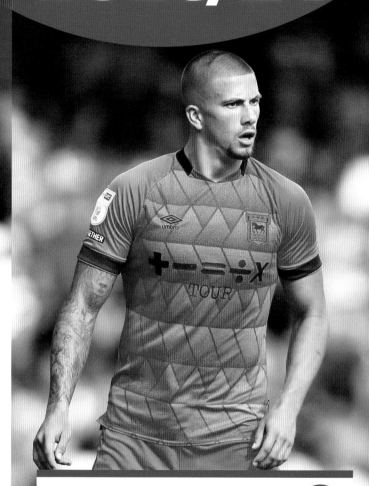

Harry
CLARKE

2

POSITION: Defender **COUNTRY:** England **DOB:** 02/03/2001

Ipswich-born Harry Clarke returned 'home' when he joined Town from Arsenal in January 2023 having previously been part of the Blues' Academy. Progressing through the Gunners' academy system, Clarke gained valuable first-team experience with loan moves to Oldham Athletic, Ross County, Hibernian and Stoke City. With the ability to play at right-back or as a central defender, Clarke provides boss Kieran McKenna with several defensive options.

Leif
DAVIS
3

POSITION: **Defender**   COUNTRY: **England**   DOB: **31/12/1999**

Left-back Leif Davis was signed from Leeds United in the summer of 2022. Town's success last season saw him celebrate back-to-back promotions, having also featured in AFC Bournemouth's promotion-winning campaign from the Championship in 2021/22, before then playing a key role in Town securing the runners-up spot in League One. A reliable defender who loves to roam forward and support attacking play, the 23-year-old chipped in with three goals last season.

George
EDMUNDSON
4

POSITION: **Defender**   COUNTRY: **England**   DOB: **15/08/1997**

Central defender George Edmundson has added power and presence to the Town backline following his summer 2021 arrival from Rangers. He featured in 18 League One matches last season as Town won promotion from the third tier. Always a threat in the opposition area when he moves forward for set-play situations, Edmundson was on target in Town's away matches at Morecambe and Charlton Athletic last season.

Sam
MORSY

5

POSITION: **Midfielder**   COUNTRY: **Egypt**   DOB: **10/09/1991**

Captain Sam Morsy played in all bar two of Town's League One fixtures last season and the inspirational leader chipped in with four goals from midfield including vital winners away to Forest Green and MK Dons. The Egyptian international brings valuable Championship experience to the Town squad having previously represented Wigan Athletic, Barnsley (loan) and Middlesbrough at second tier level.

THE CHAMPIONSHIP
SQUAD
2023/24

Luke WOOLFENDEN
6

POSITION: Defender   **COUNTRY:** England   **DOB:** 21/10/1998

Now firmly established at the heart of the Town defence, Ipswich-born central defender Luke Woolfenden has emerged from the Town Academy ranks to become a stylish, confident and reliable performer. Missing just five League One fixtures in last season's promotion-winning campaign, Woolfenden scored his first goal at Championship level as Town defeated Stoke City 2-0 in their opening home game of the 2023/24 league season.

BURNS
7

POSITION: Midfielder   **COUNTRY:** Wales   **DOB:** 23/11/1994

Wes Burns has sampled great success at Portman Road following a summer 2021 arrival from Fleetwood Town. The winger was top scorer and Player of the Year in his first campaign with the club. Then last season he played a pivotal role in the club's memorable promotion-winning campaign when he weighed in with eight league goals. One of the first names on the Town teamsheet, Burns will be keen to show his worth at Championship level in 2023/24.

9

Lee
EVANS

8

POSITION: Midfielder   **COUNTRY: Wales**   **DOB: 24/07/1994**

An important and valuable member of the Town squad, midfielder Lee Evans has featured regularly in Ipswich colours following his summer 2021 signing from Wigan Athletic. Often working in partnership with skipper Sam Morsy in the centre of the Blues' midfield, Evans is another player whose previous Championship experience will be invaluable to Ipswich in the current campaign as they compete at a higher level.

Freddie
LADAPO

9

POSITION: Forward   **COUNTRY: England**   **DOB: 01/02/1993**

Forward Freddie Ladapo fired home an impressive 17 League One goals in his first season at Portman Road as Town won promotion to the Championship. Recruited from Rotherham United ahead of last season's promotion-winning campaign, Ladapo's goals and third tier experience proved priceless to Town last season. His first goal of the current campaign came in the Carabao Cup match away to Reading.

Conor CHAPLIN

10

POSITION: Forward   **COUNTRY:** England   **DOB:** 16/02/1997

Conor Chaplin was the goalscoring sensation behind Ipswich Town's 2022/23 promotion-winning season and his 26-goal campaign in League One played a major part in him landing the club's Player of the Season award at the end of a superb campaign. Signed from Barnsley in July 2021, Chaplin is a versatile and creative front-man who will certainly be a key player for Town again in the Championship over the coming months.

Marcus
HARNESS

11

POSITION: Midfielder   **COUNTRY:** Republic of Ireland   **DOB:** 24/02/1996

Blessed with the versatility to play in several attacking midfield roles, former Burton Albion and Portsmouth man Marcus Harness joined Town from the Fratton Park club in the summer of 2022. He featured in 40 League One fixtures and netted six league goals as Town won promotion in his first season at Portman Road. The 27-year-old will be hopeful that positive performances in the Championship could lead to international recognition with the Republic of Ireland.

Dominic
BALL

12

POSITION: Midfielder   **COUNTRY:** England   **DOB:** 02/08/1995

Dom Ball joined Town ahead of last season's promotion-winning campaign after agreeing a two-year deal at Portman Road having previously been at Queens Park Rangers. With the ability to operate in midfield or in defence, Ball's flexibility is of great value to boss Kieran McKenna and the coaching staff. Despite suffering a serious knee injury last season, he still featured in 16 League One matches and netted his first goal for the Blues in our Football League Trophy match against Arsenal's U21 side.

Cieran
SLICKER
13

POSITION: Goalkeeper   **COUNTRY:** Scotland   **DOB:** 15/09/2002

A product of the Manchester City academy, goalkeeper Cieran Slicker agreed a three-year deal at Portman Road in July 2023 ahead of Town's return to the Championship. A Scotland U21 international, Slicker gained useful first-team experience with loan move to Rochdale last season when he featured in three cup fixtures for the Spotland club. His Town debut came in the 2-0 Carabao Cup first round victory over Bristol Rovers at Portman Road in August 2023.

Jack
TAYLOR
14

POSITION: Midfielder   **COUNTRY:** Republic of Ireland   **DOB:** 25/06/1998

Attacking midfielder Jack Taylor joined Ipswich Town in June 2023 as the club bolstered its squad ahead of their return to Championship football. A standout performer for Peterborough United following a January 2020 move from Barnet, Taylor netted 22 goals in 138 outings for Posh while gaining the reputation as one of the hottest talents in League One. A former Republic of Ireland U21 international, Taylor marked his Town debut with a goal in the Carabao Cup victory over Bristol Rovers.

Cameron
BURGESS
15

POSITION: Defender **COUNTRY:** Australia **DOB:** 21/10/1995

A brave, committed, and consistent central defender, Cameron Burgess has been a tower of strength at the heart of the Town defence ever since joining from Accrington Stanley in August 2021. A promotion-winner in his second season in Suffolk, Burgess started all four of the club's opening Championship matches in August 2023 as Kieran McKenna's men made an impressive start to life back in the second tier.

Brandon
WILLIAMS
18

POSITION: Defender **COUNTRY:** England **DOB:** 03/09/2000

Full-back Brandon Williams reunited with his former Manchester United coach Kieran McKenna in August 2023 when he agreed to a season-long loan at Portman Road. Capped by England at under-20 and under-21 level while progressing through the ranks at Manchester United, Williams' preferred role is at left-back, but he is equally as comfortable operating on the opposite flank. Williams has played Premier League football for both his parent club and Town's rivals Norwich City with whom he was loaned to in 2021/22.

Kayden
JACKSON 19

POSITION: **Forward** COUNTRY: **England** DOB: **22/02/1994**

Speedy and versatile frontman Kayden Jackson has now amassed over 150 appearances for Ipswich Town following his 2018 arrival from Accrington Stanley. Initially operating as an out-and-out striker, Jackson has seen his role tweaked by Kieran McKenna who tends to use Jackson's pace in wider attacking areas. The 29-year-old netted his first goal of the 2023/24 Championship campaign in Town's 2-0 victory over Stoke City at Portman Road in August.

Omari
HUTCHINSON 20

POSITION: **Midfielder** COUNTRY: **Jamaica** DOB: **29/10/2003**

Omari Hutchinson is a highly skilful and creative midfielder who joined Town on a season-long loan from Chelsea ahead of the 2023/24 Championship campaign. Turning 20 in October 2023, Hutchinson has already twice represented the full Jamaican national team. He also tasted Premier League action with Chelsea having debuted against champions Manchester City last season. A real livewire winger, Hutchinson is sure to have the Town fans on the edge of their seats this season.

THE CHAMPIONSHIP
SQUAD
2023/24

Sone
ALUKO
23

POSITION: Forward   **COUNTRY: Nigeria**   **DOB: 19/02/1989**

Former Nigerian international forward Sone Aluko provides a great deal of experience to the Town squad and is now in his third season at Portman Road. The much-travelled 34-year-old made 14 appearances in last season's promotion success and his positive influence on younger members of the squad should not be underestimated. He opened his scoring account for 2023/24 with the second goal in the Carabao Cup first round victory over Bristol Rovers.

Dane
SCARLETT
24

POSITION: Forward   **COUNTRY: England**   **DOB: 24/03/2004**

Teenage striker Dane Scarlett became the latest member of the Town squad when he agreed a season-long loan deal from Premier League Tottenham Hotspur at the end of the summer transfer window. A prolific goalscorer in academy football, Scarlett has already featured in Spurs' first-team and has also represented England at various youth levels. He spent 2022/23 on loan with League One Portsmouth and netted against Town in the EFL Trophy last season.

IPSWICH TOWN
FOOTBALL CLUB

Massimo
LUONGO
25

POSITION: Midfielder   **COUNTRY:** Australia   **DOB:** 25/09/1992

Experienced Australian international midfielder Massimo Luongo is currently in his second spell with Ipswich Town having previously played on loan for Town from Tottenham Hotspur in 2012. Initially agreeing a short-term deal at Portman Road in January 2023, he then put pen to paper on a one-year contract after impressing during the later stages of the promotion-winning campaign having been on target in victories over Shrewsbury Town and Exeter City.

Elkan
BAGGOTT

26

POSITION: Defender   **COUNTRY:** Indonesia   **DOB:** 23/10/2002

Young central defender Elkan Baggott has progressed through the Ipswich Town Academy to impress at first-team level. An Indonesian international, Baggott has enhanced his first-team experience with loan spells at National League King's Lynn and in the EFL with time spent at Gillingham and Cheltenham Town. The towering central defender will now look to obtain more game time under Kieran McKenna's watch in 2023/24.

George
HIRST

27

POSITION: Forward   **COUNTRY:** England   **DOB:** 15/02/1999

Striker George Hirst made a welcome return to Portman Road on a permanent basis in July 2023 having scored six goals while on loan from Leicester City in the second half of the 2022/23 season. A powerful and mobile frontman, Hirst agreed a four-year deal with Town and picked up from where he left off last season by scoring in Town's opening weekend 2-1 victory away to Sunderland.

SQUAD
2023/24

Cameron
HUMPHREYS **30**

POSITION: Midfielder **COUNTRY:** England **DOB:** 30/10/2003

Cameron Humphreys has progressed through the club's successful youth Academy and made his first-team debut in August 2021. The 2022/23 season proved to be a real breakthrough campaign for Humphreys with him making 26 appearances in all competitions and netting three goals. His impressive performances saw him sign a new contract with the club last season that commits him to Town until the summer of 2026.

Vaclav
HLADKY **31**

POSITION: Goalkeeper **COUNTRY:** Czech Republic **DOB:** 14/11/1990

Town recruited Czech goalkeeper Vaclav Hladky from League Two Salford City in the summer of 2021. The experienced stopper provided excellent back-up and competition to Christian Walton in the 2022/23 promotion-winning season while also making nine appearances in cup competitions. With injury ruling Walton out at the start of the current Championship campaign, Hladky proved an able deputy and recorded back-to-back clean sheets in the early season victories over Stoke City and Queens Park Rangers.

Nick
HAYES

32

POSITION: Goalkeeper   **COUNTRY: England**   **DOB: 10/04/1999**

Nick Hayes is another member of Town's goalkeeping ranks having returned to the club in January 2022 from non-league Hemel Hempstead Town. The Essex-born stopper began his youth career with Town and spent a six-month spell with Salford in the 2020/21 season having previously been on the books of Woking. The 24-year-old 'keeper is contracted to Town until the summer of 2024.

Nathan
BROADHEAD

33

POSITION: Forward   **COUNTRY: Wales**   **DOB: 05/04/1998**

Town's ambitious signing of highly-rated forward Nathan Broadhead from Everton in January 2023 proved to be the final piece of the promotion puzzle. Welsh international Broadhead hit the ground running upon his arrival at Portman Road and netted eight goals in 19 League One outings as Town ended their four-season stay in the third tier. Broadhead clearly has a major part to play in Town's 2023/24 Championship campaign and began the season in fine form with two league goals in the opening month of the season.

THE CHAMPIONSHIP
SQUAD
2023/24

Axel TUANZEBE **40**

POSITION: Defender **COUNTRY:** England **DOB:** 14/11/1997

Defender Axel Tuanzebe joined Town a week after the summer transfer window closed, arriving as a free agent and signing a one-year deal. He had been with Manchester United since the age of eight, representing the Red Devils in Premier League and Champions League games, while also captaining the senior team in an EFL Cup match against Rochdale. He brings good experience to Town, having won promotion to the Premier League with Aston Villa while also representing Stoke City and Italian side Napoli.

Janoi DONACIEN **44**

POSITION: Defender **COUNTRY:** St Lucia **DOB:** 03/11/1993

Now one of Town's longest serving players among the current squad, defender Janoi Donacien enjoyed an impressive 2022/23 campaign when he made 38 appearances in Town's promotion-winning season. His adaptability and commitment to the cause remain highly valued by boss Kieran McKenna with Donacian featuring in Town's opening three Championship games of the new season. He first joined the Blues on loan from Accrington Stanley in the summer of 2018, before making the move a permanent arrangement in the 2019 January transfer window.

ONE OF THE HARDEST THINGS TO DO IN FOOTBALL IS TO STICK THE BALL IN THE BACK OF THE NET.

NOT LEAST BECAUSE THERE ARE USUALLY ELEVEN OTHER PLAYERS TRYING TO STOP YOU DOING JUST THAT!

SHOOTING

FROM DISTANCE

Good service is obviously important, and a good understanding with your striking partner is also vital, but when it comes to spectacular strikes, practice is the key to hitting a consistently accurate and powerful shot and to developing the timing and power required.

EXERCISE

A small-sided pitch is set up with two 18-yard boxes put together, but the corners of the pitch are cut off as shown in the diagram. There are five players per team, including goalkeepers, but only one player is allowed in the opponent's half.

The aim of the drill is to work a shooting opportunity when you have the ball, with the likely chance being to shoot from outside your opponent's penalty area, from distance. The teams take it in turns to release the ball into play from their own 'keeper - usually by rolling out to an unmarked player.

18 YDS

KEY FACTORS

1. Attitude to shooting - be positive, have a go!
2. Technique - use laces, hit through the ball.
3. Do not sacrifice accuracy for power.
4. Wide angle shooting - aim for the far post.
5. Always follow up for rebounds!

SOCCER SKILLS

The size of the pitch can be reduced for younger players, and it should be noted that these junior players should also be practicing with a size 4 or even a size 3 ball, depending on their age.

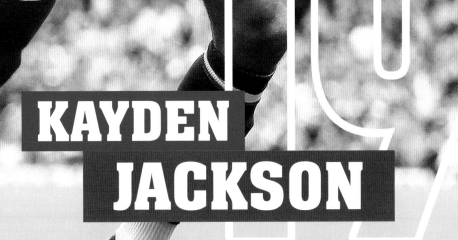

KAYDEN JACKSON

19

ITFC WOMEN

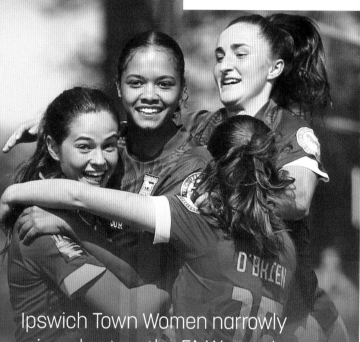

Ipswich Town Women narrowly missed out on the FA Women's National League Southern Premier Division title in 2022/23, finishing runners-up to Watford only on goal difference.

The Tractor Girls put together an impressive run of 10 consecutive victories at the end of the campaign, but a 1-0 win over Oxford United on the final day of the season was not quite enough to secure top spot. Watford went on to win promotion to the Women's Championship after beating Nottingham Forest of the Northern Premier Division 1-0 in the Championship Play-Off.

Joe Sheehan's side were consistent throughout 2022/23, winning 17, drawing two and losing just three league games. There were high scoring victories over Cheltenham Town Women (8-0), Milton Keynes Dons Women (5-1) and a trio of 3-0 wins over Crawley Wasps Ladies, London Bees and Plymouth Argyle Women.

Their home form was particularly impressive with Town 'keeper Sarah Quantrill keeping nine clean sheets at the AGL Arena as she went on to claim the FA Women's National League Awards' top goalkeeper gong at the end of the season.

In the FA Women's National League Cup qualifying round, Town thrashed Queens Park Rangers Women 7-0 in September 2022, but were defeated 2-0 by Hashtag United in the first round in November to exit the competition.

The Tractor girls scored an impressive 17 goals with no reply in the first three rounds of the Women's FA Cup. Luton Town were beaten 7-0 in round one, they put three past London Seaward in the second round and scored another seven against Portishead Town in the third round in December 2022. They could not keep up the momentum though, losing 1-0 to Lewes in the fourth round of the competition in January 2023.

Freya Godfrey, who joined Town on a dual-registration deal from Arsenal in September 2022, was Town's top goalscorer in 2022/23 with eight goals and four assists in just 16 appearances before returning to North London, and at the club's end of season awards, Megan Wearing was voted Ipswich Town's Women's Player of the Season.

DAZZLING
DEFENDERS

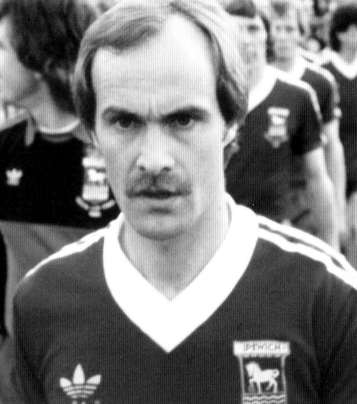

MICK MILLS, GEORGE BURLEY AND TERRY BUTCHER WERE ALL OUTSTANDING BLUES DEFENDERS AND CONTINUING THAT TRADITION IS CURRENT HOME-GROWN HERO LUKE WOOLFENDEN.

George Burley enjoyed a highly successful managerial career at Portman Road after playing 500 times for the club between 1973 and 1985.

Burley made the right-back birth his own during his playing days and was a member of 1978 FA Cup-winning team, but injury sadly ruled him out of Town's 1981 UEFA Cup success over AZ Alkmaar.

After later playing for Sunderland and Gillingham before returning north of the border to end his playing career, Burley became Town manager in November 1994. As boss he oversaw promotion to the Premier League in 2000 via the Play-Offs and then guided Town to fifth place in the Premier League in 2000/01.

Mick Mills is Town's record appearance maker and was club captain during the club's most successful era.

Holding legendary status among the Town faithful, he made a total of 741 appearances for the club over a 16-year career at Portman Road having made his debut in a 5-2 victory over Wolverhampton Wanderers back in 1966.

His many career highlights included captaining Town to FA Cup glory in 1978 and UEFA Cup success in 1981. Mills was also a regular for England at international level and captained the country during the 1982 World Cup finals in Spain.

MICK MILLS

DATE OF BIRTH: 4 January 1949

PLACE OF BIRTH: Godalming, Surrey

NATIONALITY: English

IPSWICH TOWN APPEARANCES: 741

IPSWICH TOWN GOALS: 30

IPSWICH TOWN DEBUT: 7 May 1966
Ipswich Town 5 Wolverhampton Wanderers 2 (Second Division)

GEORGE BURLEY

DATE OF BIRTH: 3 June 1956

PLACE OF BIRTH: Cumnock, East Ayrshire

NATIONALITY: Scottish

IPSWICH TOWN APPEARANCES: 500

IPSWICH TOWN GOALS: 11

IPSWICH TOWN DEBUT: 29 December 1973
Manchester United 2 Ipswich Town 0 (First Division)

Terry Butcher was born in Singapore but raised in Lowestoft, Suffolk and after joining Ipswich Town as an apprentice he progressed to become the club's central defensive linchpin of the late 1970s through until his departure to Rangers in 1986.

Part of Town's 1981 UEFA Cup-winning team, he was twice named the club's Player of the Year in 1985 and 1986. For shear bravery and commitment to the cause, there have been few players to rival Terry Butcher's performances in an Ipswich shirt.

A colossal presence at the heart of the defence for both club and country, Butcher won 77 caps for England and scored 21 goals in 351 appearances for Town.

TERRY BUTCHER

DATE OF BIRTH:	28 December 1958
PLACE OF BIRTH:	Singapore
NATIONALITY:	English
IPSWICH TOWN APPEARANCES:	351
IPSWICH TOWN GOALS:	21
IPSWICH TOWN DEBUT:	15 April 1978

Everton 1 Ipswich Town 0 (First Division)

LUKE WOOLFENDEN

DATE OF BIRTH:	21 October 1998
PLACE OF BIRTH:	Ipswich
NATIONALITY:	English
IPSWICH TOWN APPEARANCES:	154*
IPSWICH TOWN GOALS:	2*
IPSWICH TOWN DEBUT:	8th August 2017

Luton Town 0 Ipswich Town 2 (League Cup)

*AS AT THE END OF THE 2022/23 SEASON

Luke Woolfenden is living the dream of every young Town supporter by playing professional football for his hometown club.

The Ipswich-born central defender has worked his way through the Town Academy set-up to establish himself as a first-team regular at Portman Road. A confident defender who is happy in possession and always looking to build play from the back.

Wooffenden was a standout performer in the 2022/23 promotion-winning campaign. After starting 41 League One fixtures last season, he is sure to once again be one of the first names on Kieran McKenna's teamsheet in the 2023/24 Championship campaign.

10

CONOR
CHAPLIN

FOOTY

ALL OF THESE FOOTY PHRASES ARE HIDDEN IN THE GRID, EXCEPT FOR ONE ...BUT CAN YOU WORK OUT WHICH ONE? ANSWERS ON PAGE 62

PHRASES

```
C A E S W Y V V Y B H U G N U R Y M M U D
V U Q I D E R B Y D A Y O L U R T S S U
K F A D J L G T X T F C B E I A K C F P
I B H E O T L P Z R V N M W O J I R Y A
C M O F F S I D E R U L E E D S P E Y H
M E R U E I J R D E D A Q G S H L A X C
R X E R N H A T T R I C K O I L A M R T
E I Y O W W S L S N O W R S O Z Y E Y A
D C A A Z L W S J K T K Y V K B M R T M
A A L P X A U Y H M I D F I E D A R O E
E N P T K N F W G C P L J K A M K N L H
H W E J A I L O K H A O F O H I E C G T
G A M E O F T W O H A L V E S T R N U F
N V A I A H E S L F J D U A O I U O T O
I E G B I C L A S S A C T U P F G E V N
V D G O A E E U C K S S C Y W U L Q L A
I R I R Q G M N S A C H G H D O S F G M
D V B A C K O F T H E N E T Z P X B N A
```

Back of the Net	Diving Header	Half Volley	Offside Rule
Big Game Player	Dugout	Hat-trick	One-touch
Brace	Dummy Run	Keepie Uppie	Playmaker
Class Act	Final Whistle	Man of the Match	Scissor Kick
Derby Day	Game of Two Halves	Mexican Wave	Screamer

PLAYER
OF THE SEASON

Crowd favourite Conor Chaplin was the goalscoring sensation behind Ipswich Town's 2022/23 promotion-winning campaign and his 29-goal haul played a major part in him landing the club's Player of the Season award at the end of a sensational campaign.

Chaplin, who plundered a staggering 29 in all competitions, saw 26 of his goals come in vital League One fixtures as Town ended their four-season exile in the third tier.

The 26-year-old frontman netted his first goal of the season to wrap up a 3-0 home victory over MK Dons at Portman Road in August and by the end of September he had bagged six League One goals as Town got their promotion bid off to an impressive start.

A third brace of the season came in December's 2-1 home win over Peterborough United and by the turn of the year he already had a dozen goals to his name. Further double strikes came in Portman Road victories over Morecambe, Forest Green and Burton Albion as Town battled away with Plymouth Argyle and Sheffield Wednesday for an automatic promotion place.

The ace marksman was then a hat-trick hero as he departed Portman Road with the matchball following a 6-0 thrashing of Charlton Athletic in mid-April. Fittingly it was Chaplin who opened the scoring as Town defeated Exeter City on 29 April 2023 to secure the club's promotion to the Championship.

Having proved such an important member of the Town side throughout the season and appearing in all bar one of the club's League One fixtures, Chaplin's crowning as player of the year was of little surprise.

Upon receipt of the award, Chaplin said:

"It's lovely. It's nice to have had such an impact on the team this season."

Chaplin was delighted to win the award and later in the summer the Town supporters were equally delighted to learn the news that their Player of the Year had agreed a contract extension that keeps him at Portman Road until 2026.

Carry on Conor is very much the message at Portman Road!

IPSWICH TOWN
FOOTBALL CLUB

CONOR CHAPLIN

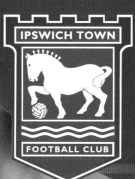

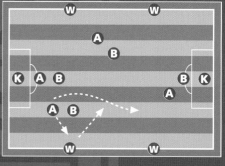

TOP CLASS PLAYERS NOT ONLY NEED TO WIN THE BALL IN MIDFIELD, BUT ALSO PROVIDE THAT CUTTING EDGE WHEN NEEDED TO BE ABLE TO PLAY THROUGH DEFENCES WITH QUICK, INCISIVE PASSING.

THE WALL PASS

With teams being very organised in modern football, it can be very difficult to break them down and create scoring opportunities. One of the best ways to achieve this is by using the 'wall pass', otherwise known as the quick one-two.

EXERCISE

In a non-pressurised situation, involving four players, A carries the ball forward towards a static defender (in this case a cone) and before reaching the defender, plays the ball to B before running around the opposite side to receive the one-touch return pass. A then delivers the ball safely to C who then repeats the exercise returning the ball to D, and in this way the exercise continues. Eventually a defender can be used to make the exercise more challenging, with all players being rotated every few minutes.

The exercise can progress into a five-a-side game, the diagram below shows how additional players (W) on the touchline can be used as 'walls' with just one touch available to help the man in possession of the ball.

Each touchline player can move up and down the touchline, but not enter the pitch - they can also play for either team.

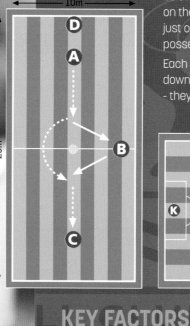

KEY FACTORS

1. Look to commit the defender before passing - do not play the ball too early.
2. Pass the ball firmly and to feet.
3. Accelerate past defender after passing.
4. Receiver (B) make themselves available for the pass.
5. B delivers a return pass, weighted correctly, into space.

SOCCER SKILLS

If done correctly, this is a tactic which is extremely difficult to stop, but needs teamwork and communication between the two attacking players.

GEORGE HIRST

27

A-Z

ARE YOU READY TO TACKLE OUR A-Z FOOTBALL QUIZ?

THE SIMPLE RULE IS THAT THE ANSWERS RUN THROUGH THE 26 LETTERS OF THE ALPHABET.

A

What nationality is Watford goalkeeper Daniel Bachmann?

A

B

Which team won the Sky Bet Championship title in 2022/23?

B

C

Which Premier League club reappointed their former manager as interim boss in March 2023?

C

D

Which League One side play their home matches at Pride Park?

D

E

What nationality is Liverpool forward Mohamed Salah?

E

F

Which country knocked England out of the FIFA World Cup finals in 2022?

F

G

Which famous football ground is due to host its final fixture in 2024?

G

H
Which club did Neil Warnock lead to Championship survival in 2022/23?

H

I
Which country did England defeat 6-2 in their opening game of the FIFA 2022 World Cup finals?

I

J
Aston Villa winger Leon Bailey plays internationally for which country?

J

K
What is the name of Premier League new boys Luton Town's home ground?

K

L
Can you name the Ipswich Town striker who netted 17 League One goals in the Tractor Boys' 2022/23 promotion-winning season?

L

M
Which Championship club boasted the division's top scorer in 2022/23?

M

ANSWERS ON PAGE 62

Q Can you name the country that hosted the FIFA 2022 World Cup finals?

Q _____

R Which Spanish side did Manchester City defeat in last season's UEFA Champions League semi-final?

R _____

S Which team knocked Premier League champions Manchester City out of the Carabao Cup last season?

S _____

N What nationality is Manchester City's ace marksman Erling Haaland?

N _____

T **Which full-back left Huddersfield Town to join Nottingham Forest ahead of their return to the Premier League in the summer of 2022?**

T _____

O Can you name the former Premier League team that will compete in the National League in 2023/24?

O _____

P Which international striker ended five seasons with Norwich City in May 2023?

P _____

X Can you name the Portuguese international defender who played in the Premier League with Everton, Liverpool & Middlesbrough?

X

Y At which club did Leeds United's Luke Ayling make his league debut?

Y

Z **Which Dutch international midfielder played Premier League football for Chelsea, Middlesbrough and Liverpool in the 2000s?**

Z

U **Can you name Brighton's German forward who joined the Seagulls in January 2022?**

U

V Can you name the former England striker who has hit over 100 Premier League goals for Leicester City?

V

W Can you name the goalkeeper who got his name on the scoresheet last season in a Championship fixture?

W

A-Z

PART TWO

IPSWICH TOWN
FOOTBALL CLUB

11

MARCUS
HARNESS

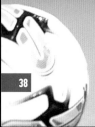

DESIGN A FOOTY BOOT

Design a brilliant new footy boot for the Town squad!

MIDFIELD
MAESTROS

JOHN WARK, JASON DOZZELL AND MATT HOLLAND WERE ALL REAL CREATORS AND SCORERS IN THE IPSWICH MIDFIELD. CONTINUING THAT FINE TOWN TRADITION IS WALES INTERNATIONAL NATHAN BROADHEAD.

Jason Dozzell is another Ipswich-born player who went on to become a true Town great, his form earning him a big money move to Tottenham Hotspur in the summer of 1993.

The attack-minded midfielder made his first-team debut on 4 February 1984 aged just 16 years and 57 days and marked the occasion with a goal in a 3-1 win over Coventry City at Portman Road.

After making 406 Tractor Boys appearances in his first spell with the club between 1984 and 1993, Dozzell returned to Portman Road from Tottenham Hotspur in 1997, making a further 10 appearances for Town. In total he scored 73 goals from midfield and played a key role in the club's 1991/92 Second Division title-winning campaign.

John Wark is a true Ipswich Town legend who amassed an incredible total of 678 appearances for the Blues over three separate spells at Portman Road.

Born in Glasgow, Wark was a goalscoring midfielder who progressed through the youth and reserve ranks to become a real star performer during the club's golden era under Sir Bobby Robson.

A member of Town's 1978 FA Cup-winning team, Wark's goals were the catalyst for the club's UEFA Cup triumph in 1981. He scored 14 goals in the competition including one in each leg of the final as Town overcame Dutch side AZ Alkmaar 5-4 on aggregate.

JOHN WARK

DATE OF BIRTH:	4 August 1957
PLACE OF BIRTH:	Glasgow, Scotland
NATIONALITY:	Scottish
IPSWICH TOWN APPEARANCES:	678
IPSWICH TOWN GOALS:	179
IPSWICH TOWN DEBUT:	27 March 1975

Ipswich Town 3 Leeds United 2 (FA Cup)

JASON DOZZELL

DATE OF BIRTH:	9 December 1967
PLACE OF BIRTH:	Ipswich
NATIONALITY:	English
IPSWICH TOWN APPEARANCES:	416
IPSWICH TOWN GOALS:	73
IPSWICH TOWN DEBUT:	4 February 1984

Ipswich Town 3 Coventry City 1 (First Division)

Matt Holland was recruited from AFC Bournemouth in the summer of 1997 for a fee of £800,000 and the midfielder became a firm crowd favourite over the six years that he was an Ipswich player.

His commitment and consistency won him many admirers and he was soon installed as captain. In 1999/2000, Holland skippered Town to promotion following the Wembley Play-Off final victory over Barnsley.

Holland starred in the Premier League in 2000/01 as Town finished fifth and he represented the Republic of Ireland at the 2002 World Cup finals. Remarkably, he missed just one league game for Town during his whole Portman Road career.

MATT HOLLAND

DATE OF BIRTH:	11 April 1974
PLACE OF BIRTH:	Bury, Lancashire
NATIONALITY:	Irish
IPSWICH TOWN APPEARANCES:	314
IPSWICH TOWN GOALS:	45
IPSWICH TOWN DEBUT:	9 August 1997

QPR 0 Ipswich Town 0 (Nationwide Division One)

NATHAN BROADHEAD

DATE OF BIRTH:	5 April 1998
PLACE OF BIRTH:	Bangor
NATIONALITY:	Welsh
IPSWICH TOWN APPEARANCES:	21*
IPSWICH TOWN GOALS:	8*
IPSWICH TOWN DEBUT:	21 January 2023

Oxford United 2 Ipswich Town 1 (League One)

*AS OF JULY 2023

Nathan Broadhead joined Town in January 2023 from Everton when he agreed a three-and-a-half year deal at Portman Road.

Emerging though the Toffees' Academy as an attacking midfielder, Broadhead gained priceless first team experience with loan spells at Burton Albion, Sunderland and Wigan Athletic.

He wasted little time in making his mark on Town's 2022/23 promotion-winning season from League One as he weighed in with eight goals in just 19 appearances as Ipswich sealed second spot. A full Wales international, the 25-year-old is expected to play a big part in Town's 2023/24 campaign back in the second tier.

CLASSIC FAN'TASTIC

Bluey is hiding in the crowd in five different places as Town fans celebrate victory in Cologne during the 1981 UEFA Cup semi-final second leg.

Can you find all five?

ANSWERS ON PAGE 62

MASSIMO LUONGO

25

15

CAMERON BURGESS

GOAL
OF THE SEASON

After scoring 26 League One goals during the club's 2022/23 promotion-winning campaign it's not surprising that it was one of top scorer Conor Chaplin's strikes that was voted Town's official Goal of the Season for 2022/23.

Kieran McKenna's free-flowing side netted a whopping 101 league goals last season and the best of the bunch was decided as being Chaplin's opening goal in the 2-0 victory over Derby County at Pride Park on 1 April 2023.

The goal capped off a stunning Town move and typified the stylish brand of possession-based attacking football that McKenna's team were playing en route to promotion.

Remarkably, this tremendous team move saw the side move the ball from goalkeeper Christian Walton's hands to the back of the Rams' the net in just eleven seconds.

From the throwout by Walton, Nathan Broadhead's run and timing to release a raking cross-field ball and then Wes Burns' cushioned header were all spot on and allowed Chaplin to finish off the move.

The goal was the leading marksman's 20th of the campaign and a perfect display of counter-attacking football at its very best. Even more importantly, it set the team on their way to another vital three points as they recorded a seventh straight League One win.

After being presented with the award at the club's end-of-season award's evening, Chaplin payed tribute to the role of his teammates in creating the opening for him to convert.

"It's a team goal for sure. I had the easy part, putting it in the back of the net. The lads before that - Walts, Broady and Wes - had a big, big part to play"

Other memorable goal in the club's promotion-winning season included George Hirst's effort on the stroke of half-time to double Town's lead in the 3-0 victory at Barsnley on 25 April. Another strong contender was Arsenal loanee Tyreece John-Jules' solo effort to open the scoring in August's 3-0 win away at Shrewsbury Town.

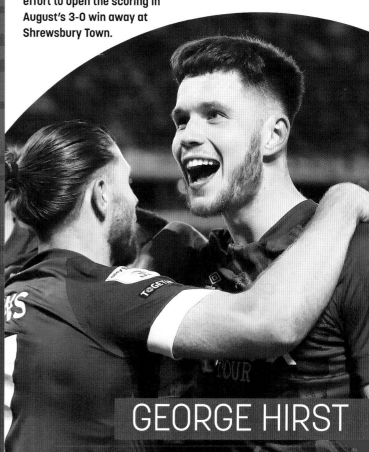

GEORGE HIRST

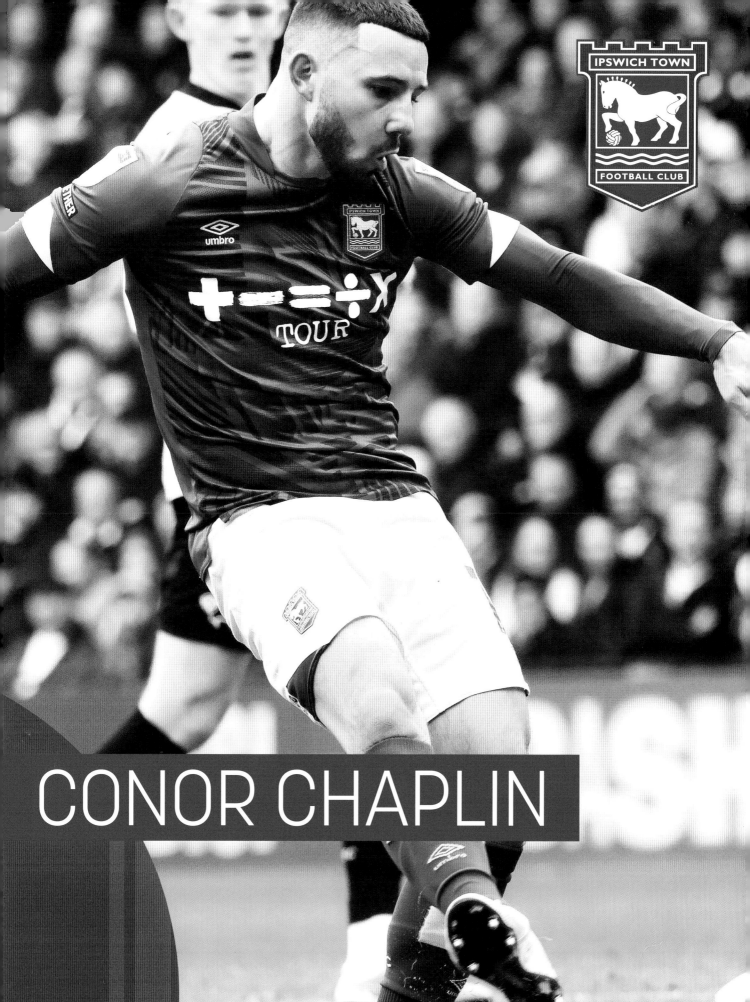

CONOR CHAPLIN

BEHIND THE

BADGE

...HIDDEN BEHIND OUR BEAUTIFUL BADGE?

A

B

C

48

D

F

G

E

H

IPSWICH TOWN
FOOTBALL CLUB

7

WES BURNS

IPSWICH TOWN
FOOTBALL CLUB

TRUE COLOURS

HAVE FUN
COLOURING
IN THIS PICTURE
OF BLUES STAR
WES BURNS

STUNNING STRIKERS

CHRIS KIWOMYA, DAVID JOHNSON AND DARREN BENT WERE ALL ACE MARKSMEN FOR IPSWICH TOWN. LOOKING TO FOLLOW IN THEIR FOOTSTEPS IS SUMMER SIGNING GEORGE HIRST.

David Johnson was a real live-wire striker that Town signed from Bury in 1997 and who enjoyed three and a half goal-laden seasons at Portman Road.

The Jamaican international netted 22 times in 37 appearances in his debut campaign with the club in 1997/98 and followed that up with 14 strikes in 1998/99 and 23 in 1999/2000. A real tricky customer in and around the penalty area, Johnson enjoyed cult status with the Town fans.

He departed for Nottingham Forest in January 2001 with an impressive goals-to-games ratio having scored a total of 62 times in 158 matches for the Tractor Boys.

Chris Kiwomya was a prolific Ipswich Town striker who hit double figures in three consecutive seasons as he netted 12 times in 1990/91 and followed that up with 19 strikes in 1991/92 and 17 in 1992/93.

A product of the club's proud youth development system in the 1980s, Kiwomya's goals proved vital in Town reaching the Premier League in 1992/93 under the management of John Lyall. His Portman Road form saw him capped by England at under-21 level.

Scoring 64 times in 261 Ipswich appearances overall, Kiwomya signed for Arsenal in January 1995. In 2008 he returned to Portman Road and worked as reserve team development coach and youth team manager.

CHRIS KIWOMYA

DATE OF BIRTH:	2 December 1969
PLACE OF BIRTH:	Huddersfield
NATIONALITY:	English
IPSWICH TOWN APPEARANCES:	261
IPSWICH TOWN GOALS:	64
IPSWICH TOWN DEBUT:	24 September 1908

Ipswich Town 1 Bradford City 1 (Division 2)

DAVID JOHNSON

DATE OF BIRTH:	15 August 1976
PLACE OF BIRTH:	Kingston, Jamaica
NATIONALITY:	Jamaican
IPSWICH TOWN APPEARANCES:	158
IPSWICH TOWN GOALS:	62
IPSWICH TOWN DEBUT:	15 November 1997

Wolves 1 Ipswich Town 1 (Nationwide Division One)

Darren Bent was yet another fantastic young talent to emerge from Town Academy set-up. The London-born striker was blessed with a great turn of speed and an expert eye for goal.

He became the focal point of Town's forward line in the early 21st century and scored 55 goals in 142 matches for the club between 2001 and 2005. He netted 20 times in 50 appearances in his final season with the Blues in 2004/05 prior to signing for then-Premier League Charlton Athletic.

Later playing top-flight football for Tottenham Hotspur, Sunderland and Aston Villa, Bent won 13 full England caps and found the back of the net on four occasions at international level.

DARREN BENT

DATE OF BIRTH:	6 February 1984
PLACE OF BIRTH:	Tooting, London
NATIONALITY:	English
IPSWICH TOWN APPEARANCES:	142
IPSWICH TOWN GOALS:	55
IPSWICH TOWN DEBUT:	1 November 2001

Helsingborg IF 1 Ipswich Town 3 (UEFA Cup)

GEORGE HIRST

DATE OF BIRTH:	5 February 1999
PLACE OF BIRTH:	Sheffield
NATIONALITY:	English
IPSWICH TOWN APPEARANCES:	23*
IPSWICH TOWN GOALS:	7*
IPSWICH TOWN DEBUT:	14 January 2023

Ipswich Town 1 Plymouth Argyle 1 (League One)

*AS AT THE END OF THE 2022/23 SEASON

George Hirst joined Ipswich Town as a permanent signing in the summer of 2023 having spent the second-half of the 2022/23 promotion-winning season on loan from Leicester City.

The striker had been a long-term Ipswich Town target and showed just why in his successful loan spell at Portman Road as be bagged his first Town goal in the FA Cup against Burnley. He then proceeded to score six times in League One as Town pipped Sheffield Wednesday to second spot.

All at Portman Road were thrilled when the club announced his permanent return to Suffolk and big things will be expected in the 2023/24 season.

REWIND

THREE GREAT IPSWICH TOWN GAMES FROM 2023

Ipswich Town 2
Sheffield Wednesday 2

SKY BET LEAGUE ONE · FEBRUARY 11, 2023

Ipswich Town battled back from two goals down to secure a vital point in what was very much League One's Match of the Day when Sheffield Wednesday visited Portman Road in February 2023.

A vital goal on the stroke of half-time from Nathan Broadhead reduced the arrears and set the tone for a thrilling second half.

The second period was just six minutes old when Leif Davis levelled to the delight of the home fans among a Portman Road crowd of 29,072.

Ipswich Town 6
Charlton Athletic 0

SKY BET LEAGUE ONE · APRIL 15, 2023

The Blues took another giant step towards promotion with an emphatic six-goal demolition of Charlton Athletic at Portman Road in April 2023.

Conor Chaplin began the rout when he gave Town a seventh-minute lead and left the stadium with the matchball having ended the afternoon with a hat-trick.

The match also saw Freddie Ladapo bag a second-half brace before Leif Davis wrapped up the scoring in the final minute.

Ipswich Town 6
Exeter City 0

SKY BET LEAGUE ONE · APRIL 29, 2023

Ipswich Town sealed their promotion to the Championship with a sensational performance at home to Exeter City.

On an afternoon of great celebration, it took Conor Chaplin just eight minutes to get the party started when he gave Town the lead. A breathtaking display of attacking football saw the hosts 5-0 up with only 32 minutes on the clock.

Wes Burns completed the scoring just two minutes after the break with the final whistle then signalling Town's promotion back to the second tier after a four-season absence.

FAST FORWARD

...AND THREE BIG CHAMPIONSHIP ENCOUNTERS TO COME IN 2024...

Leicester City (AWAY)

SKY BET CHAMPIONSHIP · JANUARY 20, 2024

One of the standout fixtures in the opening month of 2024 sees Town face Leicester City at King Power Stadium on January 20.

Since Town last faced the Foxes in the Championship, in 2013/14, Leicester City have enjoyed the most successful period in the club's history, being crowned Premier League champions in 2016 and FA Cup winners in 2021.

Relegated from the top flight at the end of last season, Leicester City will be among the favourites for an instant return to the Premier League.

Norwich City (AWAY)

SKY BET CHAMPIONSHIP · APRIL 6, 2024

Promotion from League One last season sees Ipswich return to East Anglian Derby action in 2023/24, with both local pride and Championship points at stake when we take on arch-rivals Norwich City.

One of the most eagerly-awaited fixtures of the season, Town will host the Canaries in December with the return trip to Carrow Road scheduled for April 6.

All at Portman Road will be hopeful that under the management of Kieran McKenna Town can return to winning ways this fixture. The Blues will travel to Norfolk looking for their first Carrow Road victory since 2006.

Middlesbrough (AWAY)

SKY BET CHAMPIONSHIP · APRIL 13, 2024

Defeated in the Championship Play-Off semi-finals last season, Middlesbrough are strongly fancied to challenge for promotion once again in 2023/24.

Under the guidance of former Manchester United midfielder Michael Carrick, Boro will arrive in Suffolk right at the business end of the season with just a further three games remaining.

With a real attack-minded style, which saw them score 84 league goals last season, this fixture will certainly be one of Town's tougher assignments.

BEING PREDICTABLE IS EASY IN FOOTBALL.

DOING THE UNEXPECTED IS A LOT MORE DIFFICULT.

TURNING
WITH
THE BALL

One of the biggest problems a defence can have to deal with is when a skilful player is prepared to turn with the ball and run at them, committing a key defender into making a challenge. Because football today is so fast and space so precious, this is becoming a rare skill.

EXERCISE 1

In an area 20m x 10m, A plays the ball into B who turns, and with two touches maximum plays the ball into C. C controls and reverses the process. After a few minutes the middleman is changed.

As you progress, a defender is brought in to oppose B, and is initially encouraged to play a 'passive' role. B has to turn and play the ball to C who is allowed to move along the baseline.

The type of turns can vary. Players should be encouraged to use the outside of the foot, inside of the foot, with feint and disguise to make space for the turn.

EXERCISE 2

As the players grow in confidence, you can move forward to a small-sided game. In this example of a 4-a-side practice match, X has made space for himself to turn with the ball, by coming off his defender at an angle. By doing this he can see that the defender has not tracked him, and therefore has the awareness to turn and attack.

SOCCER SKILLS

Matches at the top level are won and lost by pieces of skill such as this, so players have to be brave enough to go in search of the ball, and turn in tight situations.

IPSWICH TOWN
FOOTBALL CLUB

20

OMARI
HUTCHINSON

IPSWICH TOWN FOOTBALL CLUB

HIGH FIVES

TEST YOUR
IPSWICH TOWN
KNOWLEDGE
& MEMORY
WITH OUR
HIGH FIVES QUIZ

1. Across the previous five seasons, who have been Town's leading league goalscorers?

1. _____
2. _____
3. _____
4. _____
5. _____

3. Prior to Kieran McKenna, who were the club's last five permanent managers?

1. _____
2. _____
3. _____
4. _____
5. _____

2. Can you name Ipswich's last five FA Cup opponents ahead of the 2023/24 season?

1. _____
2. _____
3. _____
4. _____
5. _____

4. Can you name our last five EFL Cup opponents as at the end of 2022/23?

1. _____
2. _____
3. _____
4. _____
5. _____

5. Can you remember Ipswich's final league position from each of the last five seasons?

1. _____
2. _____
3. _____
4. _____
5. _____

8. Can you recall the score and season from our last five victories over rivals Norwich?

1. _____
2. _____
3. _____
4. _____
5. _____

6. Which members of the Town squad started the most league fixtures last season?

1. _____
2. _____
3. _____
4. _____
5. _____

9. Can you remember Town's last five League One victories from last season?

1. _____
2. _____
3. _____
4. _____
5. _____

7. Can you recall these players' squad No's from the 22/23 promotion-winning season?

1. Freddie Ladapo
2. Christian Walton
3. Sam Morsy
4. Leif Davis
5. Nathan Broadhead

10. Can you recall the club's end of season points tally from the last five seasons?

1. _____
2. _____
3. _____
4. _____
5. _____

SENSATIONAL STOPPERS

PAUL COOPER, RICHARD WRIGHT AND BARTOSZ BIAŁKOWSKI WERE ALL GREAT TOWN GOALKEEPERS. CONTINUING THAT PROUD TREND IS CURRENT IPSWICH STOPPER CHRISTIAN WALTON.

Richard Wright progressed through the club's youth system and the Ipswich-born goalkeeper went on to win full England recognition during his first of three spells with the club.

Part of the Town side that enjoyed Play-Off glory at Wembley in 2000, Wright then produced a string of eye-catching performances as Ipswich took the Premier League by storm. His club form was rewarded with a full England debut in the summer of 2000 and a year later he sealed a big-money move to Arsenal.

In the summer of 2008, after plying his trade at Everton and West Ham United, Wright returned to Portman Road for a second spell with the club. Then in 2011 he made a third Ipswich Town debut.

Paul Cooper began his career with Birmingham City and after 17 league matches for the St Andrew's club he joined Town in 1974 and proceeded to become a cult hero who played 575 times for Ipswich.

Cooper was an excellent all-round goalkeeper with assured handling and great reflexes, but it was his remarkable ability to save penalties that saw him become such a terrace hero. In the 1979/80 season he saved an incredible eight out of the ten spot-kicks he faced.

A member of the 1978 FA Cup-winning team and also a UEFA Cup winner in 1981, Cooper remains the Town 'keeper that all others will be judged against.

PAUL COOPER

DATE OF BIRTH:	21 December 1953
PLACE OF BIRTH:	Cannock, Staffordshire
NATIONALITY:	English
IPSWICH TOWN APPEARANCES:	575
IPSWICH TOWN DEBUT:	20 April 1974

Leeds United 3 Ipswich Town 2 (First Division)

RICHARD WRIGHT

DATE OF BIRTH:	5 November 1977
PLACE OF BIRTH:	Ipswich
NATIONALITY:	English
IPSWICH TOWN APPEARANCES:	355
IPSWICH TOWN DEBUT:	5 May 1995

Ipswich Town 2 Coventry City 0 (Premier League)

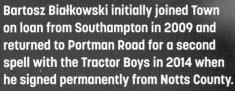

Bartosz Białkowski initially joined Town on loan from Southampton in 2009 and returned to Portman Road for a second spell with the Tractor Boys in 2014 when he signed permanently from Notts County.

The giant Polish stopper was an outstanding performer for Town and starred as Mick McCarthy's side reached the Championship Play-Offs in 2014/15. His consistent performances were rewarded with the club's Player of the Year award in three consecutive seasons from 2015/16 through to 2017/18.

Following Town's relegation in 2019, he opted to remain in the Championship when he joined Millwall, initially on loan, before completing a permanent switch to the South London side.

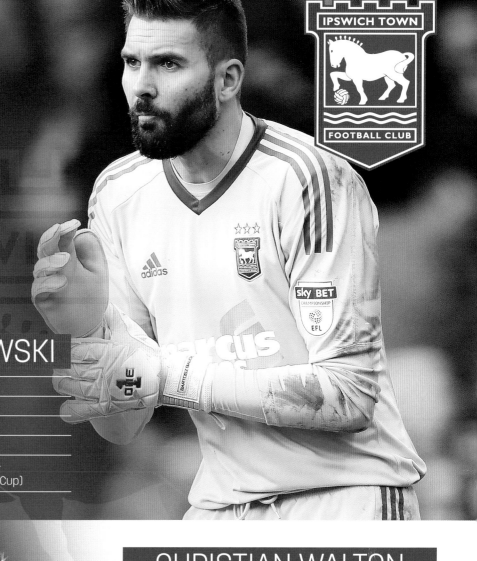

BARTOSZ BIAŁKOWSKI

DATE OF BIRTH: 6 July 1987

PLACE OF BIRTH: Braniewo, Poland

NATIONALITY: Polish

IPSWICH TOWN APPEARANCES: 178

IPSWICH TOWN DEBUT: 12 August 2014
Crawley Town 1 Ipswich Town 0 (League Cup)

CHRISTIAN WALTON

DATE OF BIRTH: 9 November 1995

PLACE OF BIRTH: Wadebridge, Cornwall

NATIONALITY: English

IPSWICH TOWN APPEARANCES: 85*

IPSWICH TOWN DEBUT: 11 September 2021
Ipswich Town 2 Bolton Wanderers 5 (League One)

*AS AT THE END OF THE 2022/23 SEASON

Christian Walton is Town's current No.1 having initially joined the Blues on loan from Premier League Brighton & Hove Albion in August 2021. Following a string of impressive performances the move was made a permanent one in the 2022 January transfer window.

A firm favourite with the Town fans and a highly-respected member of squad, Walton is a confident goalkeeper who commands his area and gives great confidence to those playing in front of him.

The reliable stopper was ever-present in Town's 2022/23 promotion-winning season from League One and is expected to have a key role to play as the club looks to establish themselves as a competitive force at Championship level in 2023/24.

ANSWERS

PAGE 29: FOOTY PHRASES

Keepie Uppie.

PAGE 34: A-Z QUIZ

A. Austrian. B. Burnley. C. Crystal Palace. D. Derby County. E. Egyptian.
F. France. G. Goodison Park (Everton). H. Huddersfield Town. I. Iran.
J. Jamaica. K. Kenilworth Road. L. Ladapo, Freddie. M. Middlesbrough
(Chuba Akpom). N. Norwegian. O. Oldham Athletic. P. Pukki, Teemu.
Q. Qatar. R. Real Madrid. S. Southampton. T. Toffolo, Harry. U. Undav,
Deniz. V. Vardy, Jamie. W. Wilson, Ben (Coventry City). X. Xavier, Abel.
Y. Yeovil Town. Z. Zenden, Boudewijn.

PAGE 42: FAN'TASTIC

PAGE 48: BEHIND THE BADGE

A. Nathan Broadhead.
B. Luke Woolfenden. C. Wes Burns.
D. Harry Clarke. E. Omari Hutchinson.
F. Kayden Jackson. G. Massimo
Luongo. H. Marcus Harness.

PAGE 58: HIGH FIVES

QUIZ 1: 1. 2022/23, Conor Chaplin
(26 goals). 2. 2021/23, Wes Burns
& Macauley Bonne (12 goals each).
3. 2020/21, James Norwood (Nine
goals). 4. 2019/20, Kayden Jackson
& James Norwood (11 goals each).
5. 2018/19, Gwion Edwards & Freddie
Sears (Six goals each)

CLASSIC
FAN'TASTIC
Bluey is hiding in the crowd in five
different places as Town fans celebrate
victory in Cologne during the
1981 UEFA Cup semi-final second leg.
Can you find all five?

QUIZ 2: 1. 2022/23 Burnley (fourth round). 2. 2022/23, Rotherham
United (third round). 3. 2022/23, Buxton (second round). 4. 2022/23,
Bracknell (first round). 5. 2021/22, Barrow (second round).

QUIZ 3: 1. Paul Cook. 2. Paul Lambert. 3. Paul Hurst. 4. Mick McCarthy.
5. Paul Jewell.

QUIZ 4: 1. Colchester United (2022/23). 2. Newport County (2021/22).
3. Fulham (2020/21). 4. Luton Town (2019/20). 5. Exeter City (2018/19).

QUIZ 5: 1. 2nd in League One (2022/23). 2. 11th in League One (2021/22).
3. 9th in League One (2020/21). 4. 11th in League One (2019/20)*.
5. 24th in Championship (2018/19)

QUIZ 6: 1. Christian Walton (46 League One starts). 2. Sam Morsy
(44 League One starts). 3. Leif Davis (43 League One starts).
4. Wes Burns, Conor Chaplin & Luke Woolfenden (all on 41 League One
starts). 5. Cameron Burgess (30 Premier League starts).

QUIZ 7: 1. 9. 2. 1. 3. 5. 4. 3. 5. 33.

QUIZ 8: 1. 2008/09, Ipswich Town 3-2 Norwich City (Championship).
2. 2007/08, Ipswich Town 2-1 Norwich City (Championship).
3. 2006/07, Ipswich Town 3-1 Norwich City (Championship).
4. 2005/06, Norwich City 1-2 Ipswich Town (Championship).
5. 2002/03, Norwich City 0 Ipswich Town 2 (Championship).

QUIZ 9: 1. Fleetwood Town 2-2 Ipswich Town.
2. Ipswich Town 6-0 Exeter City. 3. Barnsley 0-3 Ipswich Town.
4. Ipswich Town 2-1 Port Vale. 5. Ipswich Town 6-0 Charlton Athletic.

QUIZ 10: 1. 2022/23, 98 points. 2. 2021/22, 70 points.
3. 2020/21, 69 points. 4. 2019/20, 52 points**. 5. 2018/19, 31 points.

* Table decided on points-per-game basis, ** Points won before season curtailed.